Samuel Miller

A sermon, delivered February 5, 1799

Recommended by the clergy of the city of New-York

Samuel Miller

A sermon, delivered February 5, 1799
Recommended by the clergy of the city of New-York

ISBN/EAN: 9783337264819

Printed in Europe, USA, Canada, Australia, Japan

Cover: Foto ©Lupo / pixelio.de

More available books at **www.hansebooks.com**

A

SERMON,

DELIVERED FEBRUARY 5, 1799;

RECOMMENDED BY THE CLERGY OF THE CITY OF
NEW-YORK,

TO BE OBSERVED AS A DAY OF

THANKSGIVING, HUMILIATION, AND PRAYER,

ON ACCOUNT OF THE REMOVAL OF A

MALIGNANT AND MORTAL DISEASE,

WHICH HAD PREVAILED IN THE CITY
SOME TIME BEFORE.

BY SAMUEL MILLER, A. M.

ONE OF THE MINISTERS OF THE UNITED PRESBYTERIAN
CHURCHES IN THE CITY OF NEW-YORK.

PUBLISHED BY REQUEST.

NEW-YORK:

PRINTED BY GEORGE FORMAN.

1799.

A SERMON, &c.

Psalm ii. 11.

—— *Rejoice with trembling.*

To seek refuge in the power of
God, and cry to him for mercy in an hour of distress, is the language of nature as well as of grace.
When the pressure of calamity is severely felt, we
see the profane as well as the pious repairing to
the throne of the Eternal, and looking up for that
aid, which in ordinary times they neglect and des-
pise.   But, though the unbelieving and impious
are ready enough to cry for deliverance from suf-
fering, they are apt to think little of the gratitude
and duty which they owe after the mercy is received.   The character of mankind in general, too
much accords with that of the children of Israel,
which is delivered by the Psalmist—*When he slew
them, then they sought him ; and they returned and
enquired early after God : then they remembered
that God was their Rock, and the Most High their
Redeemer.   Nevertheless they did flatter him with*

their mouth, and they lied unto him with their tongue. They remembered not his hand, nor the day when he delivered them.

It is my earnest prayer, my brethren, that we may not ourselves be examples of this ungrateful and odious temper. But a few weeks have elaps- ed since we saw the most thoughtless irresistibly constrained to pause and consider ; and the most daring scoffer impelled to put up a petition for mercy to the Almighty Sovereign of the universe. The aspect of divine Providence is now changed. The voice of mirth and gladness is again heard in our social circles ; and the activity of prosperous business is again seen, where the silence and gloom of death lately prevailed. But do we come before the Most High this day, with those prompt and fervent emotions which we felt under the pres- sure of his afflicting hand ? Have we entered this house as solicitously concerned about *improving* his mercy as we lately were to *obtain* it ? Is our joy that of the humble and affectionate heart, which returns to Him who hath dealt bountifully with it ; or is it the inconsiderate confidence of those who having once escaped, think no more of the power and justice which corrected, or of the mercy which spared them ?

With a view, if possible, to stir up in your minds and my own, a temper corresponding to the solemn occasion on which we are convened, I have chosen the concise but comprehensive words which were just read.   They are taken from a Psalm, in which the inspired writer predicts desolating judgments and awful dispensations as about to take place in the course of God's dealings with the world.   As an inference from these predictions, or as an incitement to improve them, he delivers the words of our text—*Be wise now, therefore, O ye kings, be instructed, ye judges of the earth. Serve the Lord with fear, and rejoice with trembling.*

The sentiment contained in these words is obvious and important.   It is this—That we are bound, at all times, even the most distressing, to rejoice in the government of God, as holy, wise, and good ;—but, at the same time, in every season, however prosperous and flattering, to mingle fear and trembling with our joy, as dependent and sinful beings, who are continually exposed to the wrath of heaven, and who have no reason to be confident in ourselves, or to presume on present enjoyment.

In applying this passage of scripture to the solemnity in which we are engaged, it shall be my endeavor,

I. To shew the obligation which we are under to come before God, this day, with joy and praise.

II. To explain the manner in which our joy should be exercised and qualified, and the grounds of this qualification.

I. I begin with shewing the obligation which we are under to come before God, this day, with joy and praise.

That gratitude to God is a duty, no rational being, who believes that there is a God, has ever denied. If there be a sentiment in which men of all characters, and of all modes of thinking are unanimous, it is this—that we ought to cherish emotions of thankfulness towards our Almighty. Benefactor, and rejoice in his existence, his perfections, and his will. Some vain theory-builders have, indeed, contended that gratitude between man and man was not a duty; supposing it to be inconsistent with their refined and extravagant notions of justice. But I know not that even these, at least such of them as believe in the existence of a Deity, have ever called in question the duty of. gratitude to Him. They have acknowledged that here thankfulness sincere and ardent is incumbent upon us, and that to withhold it is robbing God of his just due.

The grounds of joy and praise are unnumbered and ceaseless. Every object we behold, and every moment we live, afford abundant matter for this exercise. There is no situation in which we can be placed, there is no occurrence which we can be called to contemplate, but what suggests ample reason for thankfulness and rejoicing. Hence one inspired writer declares—*I will bless the Lord at all times, his praise shall continually be in my mouth.** And another exhorts, *Rejoice in the Lord; rejoice always; and again, I say, rejoice.*†

You might, with propriety, be called upon this day, to rejoice and praise God for his beneficence in creation; for the noble faculties and powers with which we are endowed; and for the various beauties and comforts of the world in which our lot is cast. You might be called upon to rejoice and praise him for the common bounties of his Providence; for food and raiment; for numerous enjoyments of body and mind; for fruitful seasons; for the regular return of summer and winter, seed-time and harvest; and for our preservation through another year. It might be shewn that our fervent gratitude is due and demanded for social, family, and national blessings; for civil and religious liberty; for governments of our own choice, and laws of our own formation; for the peaceful enjoyment of the fruits of our labours; and for the measure of tranquility and plenty which smile around us. It might be demonstrated that we are under obligations to express our joy and praise to

* Psalms xxxiv. 1.   † Philip. iv. 4.

God even for his *judgments*; for be assured, brethren, we shall never exercise a proper temper
toward him, unless, with the Apostle, we *rejoice
in tribulation,* and give thanks for the chastenings
of his rod, as designed to work together for the
good of all who love him—as real blessings in
disguise. You might, with propriety, be exhorted, above all, to offer the sacrifices of thanksgiving for the Gospel Redemption; for the gift of an
almighty and all-sufficient Saviour; for enlarging
our views beyond these regions of disorder and
darkness; for the new Covenant, established upon
glorious promises, and containing all our salvation
and all our desire. Especially are the gospel of
Christ, and the continuance of our spiritual privile-
ges proper subjects of social thanksgiving at the present day, when their opposers are more than com-
monly numerous and bold; when they display a
zeal unwearied and malignant to bring the doc-
trines, the duties, and the teachers of this holy religion into contempt; and when they publicly
glory in the expectation of its speedy downfal.
How much reason have we, christians! for un-
feigned gratitude, that, amidst so much secret
and open opposition, the cause of our divine Mas-
ter lives and triumphs; that his sabbaths continue
to be, by a goodly portion of our citizens, observed and honored; that his ordinances are respect-
fully attended; that his messengers are still sent
forth to proclaim the good news of salvation to

guilty men ; and that every day furnishes encreasing ground of confidence · that the gates of hell shall never prevail against his church, but that He will reign until He put all enemies under his feet !

But passing over these various topics of grateful acknowledgment, not because they are unworthy of more particular notice, but because they equally demand at all times the most affectionate ascriptions of praise—I would direct your attention to that special ground of joy and humble gratitude, which led to the appointment on which we are now convened—THE DIVINE GOODNESS IN DELIVERING US FROM THE RAVAGES OF PESTILENCE, which lately cloathed our city with the mantle of mourning.

There are, probably, few cases in which we feel ourselves more completely helpless, and more entirely in the hands of God, than when He sends forth pestilence, as a messenger of his wrath to chastise a guilty society ; when the atmosphere which we breathe bears in its component materials the seeds of dissolution and death ; when the weapons of destruction float around us unseen, and the fell destroyer presents no tangible front, to which we can oppose our strength and our feeble devices. Then it is, if ever, that human pride bows its head :—then, if ever, that the incorrigible infidel thinks, for a moment, of a God, of Providence, and of prayer.

Have you forgotten, my brethren, that such was lately our situation? Have you forgotten the calamity, which, a few weeks ago, ravaged our city, which filled your hearts with consternation, and covered your faces with paleness? Have you forgotten the memorable period, when the king of terrors raised his bloody standard in the midst of us, and waved it triumphant through all our streets; when with his destroying sword he hewed down our neighbours and friends, sparing neither sex, condition, nor age; when with merciless looks and contagious breath, he walked, amidst the gloom of midnight and the light of noon-day, laying victim after victim at his feet? Have you forgotten the period when this grim tyrant defied all the forces which the wisdom and power of man could bring against him; when he knocked at almost every door, demanding, with imperious voice, sometimes one, and sometimes two victims in a house, and sometimes with undistinguishing fury, bearing away every member of the fond domestic circle, leaving no survivor to deplore his melancholy ravages, or to tell the tale of woe? Have you forgotten those gloomy days, when scarcely any sound was heard, but the voice of mourning and death; when few passengers were seen, save the bearers of putrefying mortality to the tomb ; when the labours of the artizan and the speculations of the merchant were suspended ; and when the means of splendid adorning were exchanged for the coffin, the shroud, and the grave ? Have you forgotten the anguish which you felt, through sympathy for the afflictions of others, and through apprehension for your own safety ? Have you forgotten the vows which you made, and the resolutions which you formed in those serious and solemn hours ? No, you cannot have forgotten scenes and feelings such as these. Had your own memories been unable to retain them, the numberless monuments and memorials which surround you, would recal them continually to your minds. The badges of mourning which I see before me, bring to my remembrance, a husband or a wife, a parent or a child, a brother or a sister recently torn from your embraces, and consigned to the insatiable tomb. O Death! how large the catalogue of thy trophies ! what inroads hast thou made on the arrangements and peace of families, and on the endearments of social life !

Brethren, I have not drawn this picture with a view to harrow up your feelings, or to wound those tender sensibilities which I perceive to be excited in your bosoms :—but from a wish to impress you with a deep sense of your obligation to God for the happy change, which his mercy has produced in the state of our city. Bereaved and afflicted hearers ! weep not as those who have no hope ! Believe in HIM who is *the Resurrection and the Life*, and who has promised, when He comes again, to bring with him in glory, all who have fallen asleep in the faith of his gospel.

But to whom are we indebted for the removal of that calamity, which has been so inadequately described ? Surely not to human ingenuity or human strength. How often did we see the prudent precaution useless, and the studied care of the wise put to shame ! How often did we see the most plausible plans of prevention fail, and the most promising theories of medical wisdom demolished, or set at nought by the subtle destroyer ! Yes, brethren, in the preservation of each of us, there is the finger of God. Some he saved by providing a place of refuge, where the salubrious breeze, and the hospitable board sustained them till the evil was past ; while others were preserved though walking in the midst of the devouring poison, to discharge the duties of benevolence and humanity. Nor was the hand of God less visible in arresting the progress of the destructive malady, than in guarding our lives amidst its raging power. When the survivors were helpless, and apprehended a devastation still more awful, He appeared to stay the plague. When there was no earthly power to whom we could look for safety, and when the experience of every day proved that human aid was vain, then did the great Physician interpose with his healing power. He dispelled the malignant vapours which enveloped our habitations. He ordered the season in mercy; and in due time restored the voice of joy, and the activity of business, to our lately deserted dwellings.

I shall not stay here, to combat the objections of those who may contend—" That this deliverance has been brought about by mere natural causes, without God; and that to ascribe it to divine agency, or a particular Providence is weak and superstitious." With respect to those who adopt this language, I would only ask them—What is *nature* without GOD? What do you call by this name, but the ordinary method in which Jehovah actuates and guides the material world? Is it not *by the breath of his mouth that frost is given?* Is it not by his command that *cold cometh out of the north?* Doth he not *say to the rain—Be thou on the earth?* Doth he not regulate all these, *that they may do whatsoever he commandeth them on the face of the earth, either for correction, or for mercy?** And is it not acknowledged to be by the secondary influence of these causes, that the progress of pestilence is arrested, and its virulence destroyed? Philosophy! I venerate thy name! In

* Job xxxvii. 6—15.

the simple garb of truth, and as the humble inter-
preter of Jehovah's works, thou art the handmaid
of religion, and the friend of virtue. But when
corrupted and deformed with the gaudy trappings
of human folly; when, with presumptuous hands,
thou wouldst invade the throne of God; when thou
wouldst hide from man the wisdom and power by
which he exists, thou becomest the enemy of
sound reason, and the foe of human happiness!

*Give unto the Lord, therefore, O ye people, give
unto the Lord glory and strength. Give unto the
Lord the glory that is due unto his name.* He
hath not dealt with us after our sins, nor rewarded
us according to our iniquities.† He hath torn, and
he hath healed; he hath smitten, and he hath bound
us up.‡ Like as a father pitieth his children, so
hath he pitied and spared us. He remembered our
frame, he remembered that we were but dust. Bless
the Lord, O our souls; and all that is within us,
bless his holy name. Bless the Lord, O our souls,
and forget not all his benefits; who healeth our diseases; who redeemeth our lives from destruction;
who crowneth us with loving-kindness and tender
mercies.§*

Having made these remarks on the grounds of
that joy and praise which we are called this day to
render, I shall attempt,

---

* Psa. xxxix. 1, 2.   † Psa. ciii. 11.   ‡ Hos. 6. 1.
§ Psa. ciii. 1—14.

II. To explain the manner in which our joy should be exercised and qualified, and the reasons of this qualification. *Rejoice with trembling.*

There are few things to which human nature is more prone than presumptuous confidence :—And there are, perhaps, few occasions on which it is more apt to appear, than in the first transports of joy, on being delivered from the pressure of calamity, or from the dread of impending danger. Of the truth of this remark the sacred history abounds with examples. In almost every instance in which, the children of Israel emerged from the overwhelming judgments, which their sins brought upon them, they are represented immediately after, as becoming more proud and self-confident than ever ; more forgetful of the hand of their Deliverer ; and more bold transgressors of his righteous law. And in like manner, has it been found, from that period to the present day, that *the prosperity of fools destroys them.* Hence the propriety and importance of the exhortation in our text—*Serve the Lord with fear, and rejoice with trembling.*

By the *trembling* inculcated in this place, we are not to understand that *servile fear* and *pusillanimous dread,* which rather become those *who have no hope, and are without God in the world.* Neither are we to consider it as diminishing our sense of favors received, or as at all inconsistent with the utmost fervor of gratitude. But the expression implies, that our joy should be mingled with such an humble sense of dependance ; with such an awful conviction of our demerit in the sight of an holy God ; and with such a solemn impression that we are still in his hands, as will repress arrogance and pride, and teach us to maintain the spirit of filial fear. The language of the exhortation, in short, is this—" Children of the dust ! let not your joy be the exulting levity, or the inconsiderate confidence of those who, in prosperity, imagine their mountain will forever stand strong. But let all your thanksgiving be mingled with humility, and all your joy tempered with the recollection, that sinful beings are continually exposed to wrath and chastisement, and have no ground of security in themselves."

Among many considerations which might be urged to qualify our joy this day, and mingle with it an holy trembling, permit me to select and lay before you the following.

1. We have reason to tremble, lest the judicial dispensation of Providence, for the removal of which we this day rejoice, should not be SANCTIFIED. The judgments of God are frequently represented in scripture, under the strong and striking figure of a *furnace*, designed to try and purify that which is subjected to its power. They are intended,

like the refiner's process, to separate from us our
moral corruption; to purge from our hearts and
our manners whatever is base and pernicious.
Now we are uniformly assured, by the same Divine Authority which gives us this view of the subject, that if they fail of producing this spiritual pu-
rification in our tempers and lives, we shall come
out of them more obdurate, and at a greater dis-
tance from the hope of reformation than before.—
When a remedy is applied to the natural constitu-
tion of man, if a frequent repetition of it be demanded by the obstinacy of the disease, the physician finds its efficacy to become daily less and less;
he observes the system to become more insensible
of its influence, in proportion to the frequency and
length of the application; until at length the larg-
est portion he can exhibit will produce but little
effect.   Thus it is with the human heart, with
respect to the judicial dispensations of Providence.
They are moral remedies, for moral diseases.
They are intended to operate a deep and effectual
conviction of the holiness of God, and of his displeasure against sin; to cloathe us with humility,
and lead us to repentance—This is the sanctified
use of them which it is our duty to make.   But
where they fail of producing these effects, they
leave the heart more insensible, the conscience
more seared, the ears more deaf to the voice of
heaven, the eyes more blind to truth and duty,

C .

and the whole man lying under an additional load
of guilt, and at a farther remove from the kingdom
of God.

To all those who enter into these views of the
subject, it will appear neither a novel nor an un-
justifiable assertion to pronounce—That, if the
affliction from which we have been recently delivered, be not sanctified, the very deliverance in
which we now rejoice, will but increase our guilt
and our danger. If the dispensation do not produce *the peaceable fruits of righteousness*, it will
leave us a more hardened and stiff-necked people
—at a greater remove from penitence—and ripe
for higher tokens of the divine displeasure. *My
spirit*, says God, *shall not always strive with man.
He that being often reproved, hardeneth his neck,
shall suddenly be cut off, and that without remedy.
Because I have called, and ye refused; I have
stretched out my hand, and no man regarded; but
ye have set at nought all my counsel, and would
none of my reproof: I also will laugh at your calamity; I will mock when your fear cometh; when
your fear cometh as desolation, and your destruction cometh as a whirlwind; when distress and anguish cometh upon you.—Then shall they call upon
me, but I will not answer; they shall seek me early,
but they shall not find me: For that they hated
knowledge and did not chuse the fear of the Lord:
They would none of my counsel; they despised all*

my reproof. Therefore shall they eat the fruit of their own ways, and be filled with their own devices.*

From these passages of the sacred volume, you will observe, that the evils to be apprehended from unsanctified afflictions, are of two kinds ; either being visited with more overwhelming judgments ; or, being given up to judicial hardness. Of the first of these I shall afterwards speak. With respect to the second, however little it may be dreaded by the infidel and the formalist, it will appear no inconsiderable thing to the serious believer in God's word. Or rather, to speak more properly, it will appear to such an one, the greatest and most dreadful of all judicial dispensations. Spiritual judgments, though less observed, and usually less alarming in their aspect, than those which strike at our mortal existence, and our temporal interests, ought undoubtedly to be viewed by reasonable beings as a thousand fold more just objects of terror than they. Deplorable, indeed, is the condition of that people to whom God says —*Why should ye be stricken any more ? Ye will revolt more and more. They are joined to idols ; let them alone !* Such a people may exult, and bless themselves in their abundant wealth. They may be the envy of their neighbours, and may construe the forbearance of God into smiles of love.

* Prov. i. 24—32.

They may be safe from foreign invasion and from predatory violence. Their cities may not be burnt with fire, nor wasted with disease. Their fields may not be blasted with mildew, nor their precious fruits destroyed by the locust or the caterpillar. Their commerce, agriculture, and manufactures may flourish; and many a short-sighted beholder may pronounce them blessed. But their prosperity rests upon a deceitful basis. Above, the tempest is gathering unseen. Beneath, the volcano is accumulating its dreadful materials, and hastening to the exploding hour. And in an unexpected moment, when they are saying *peace and safety to themselves,* sudden desolation shall overtake them—a desolation the more aggravated in proportion to its delay. Do you ask for an example? Look at the history of the Jews. Being found, after many chastisements, altogether incorrigible, God *gave them up to their own hearts' lusts, and left them to walk in their own counsels, until they had filled up the measure of their iniquities, and wrath came upon them to the uttermost.* Then their national sovereignty was taken away; their capital was destroyed; and they were scattered abroad, bearing in every place, the stamp of divine displeasure, being made *an hissing, and a bye-word among all nations.*

How much reason have we to tremble, then, lest our deliverance should be sent in wrath; lest

-what we celebrate as a blessing, may be converted by human folly into a curse ; lest, with respect to many, their songs of joy, should prove the chauntings of devoted victims, on the altar of their own destruction !

2. While we come before God with joy and praise, for the merciful deliverance, which we this day commemorate, it becomes us to tremble lest we should be again visited by a similar, or a more dreadful calamity. You have heard, that when the judgments which God executeth are not sanctified, if he do not immediately cast off the subjects of his chastisement, they may expect farther and heavier strokes of his rod. They may expect one visitation after another, each in succession more dreadful, until the great end of humbling and reforming them be obtained.

Brethren, let not self-flattery hide from your eyes the danger which lies before you. Indulge not the sanguine hope, that, because the tremendous scourge has again passed over, you will be secure from its ravages in future. It is my fervent wish and prayer that this may prove to be the case ; but this enlightened audience will excuse me for expressing doubts and fears, that such complete exemption can hardly be expected. *Wheresoever the carcase is, there will the eagles be gathered together.**

* Matt. xxiv. 28.

Where so many natural and moral causes of public calamity exist, it would be almost a miracle were we to escape the judgments of God. While our city and. land groan under so much depravity. and corruption, we have too much reason to fear, that they will also be made to groan under encreasing, and more destructive testimonies of the divine displeasure.

I say not this, my beloved hearers, to discourage, or unduly to alarm you ; but to encrease your solicitude, and to animate your diligence in using the means of prevention, which Providence has put into your-hands. With respect to one class of these preventives, I mean those of a *natural* or *physical* kind, it would be foreign from my duty, at present, to enter into details, or to offer opinions, farther than to express a firm belief, that such may be found ; that there is much in.this respect, humanly speaking, in our power ; and that it would be criminal negligence to pass them by. But with regard to another class of preventives, I mean those of a *moral* or *spiritual* kind; it would be injustice both to you, and to my subject, to pass them over in silence. Bear with me, then, my brethren, while I express a persuasion, painful indeed, to utter, but which a regard to truth extorts from me—That God has a controversy with us, and that reformation is the only mean of escaping his consuming. wrath. While so much corruption, blasphemy, and wickedness triumph in the midst of us, and insult his holiness, to hope for his smiles, is to contradict every declaration of his word. While this continues to be our character, we may expect scourges and judgments, as certainly as we expect the return of summer and winter, seed-time and harvest. Infinite wisdom only can tell whether pestilence, or famine, or war will be the instrument of his wrath ; or at how long or short intervals, these judicial dispensations may occur ; but of this, every page of scripture warrants us in being confident, that, on the one hand, were we an holy people, we should seldom or never hear of such destroying calamities ; but that, on the other hand, if our guilt and corruption, as a people go on and accumulate, we may anticipate the time when these will be more frequent, extensive, and dreadful than they have ever yet been. In support of what is here advanced, the sacred volume furnishes abundant proof and example. Overwhelming judgments were denounced by Jehovah against Nineveh, for its great and crying wickedness. *And the people of Nineveh believed God, and proclaimed a fast, and put on sackcloth, from the greatest even to the least ; and they cried mightily unto him, and turned every one from the evil of his way, and from the violence that was in their hands—saying—Who can tell if God will turn and repent, and turn away from his fierce anger that we perish not ? And God saw their works, that they*

*turned from their evil way ; and God repented of
the evil that he had said he would do unto them, and
he did it not.** So much for a favorable issue, in the
case of a penitent people. But turn for a moment
to a signal and melancholy instance of an oppo-
site kind. Jerusalem was highly favored of God.†
His smiles upon her were peculiar and long. His
warnings, when she went astray, were numerous. His paternal chastisements and affectionate
calls, to bring her to a sense of duty, were conti-
nued from year to year, and from age to age.
When lighter judgments were found ineffectual,
greater and heavier were laid upon her, in awful
succession ; until, at length, proving incorrigibly
obstinate, she was rejected ; her glory finally de-
parted ; and she was delivered up to a ruin, which
for accumulated horrors, has scarcely a parallel in
the history of man.

Let none say, that placing *moral reformation*
among the principal preventives of future calamities similar to that which we have lately sustained,
is discarding the agency of second causes. I
would by no means be understood to do this.

---

* Jonah iii. 5. ad fin.

† It will readily occur to the reader, that although this
people were adduced to illustrate a former branch of the
subject, their case may, with equal propriety, be again men-
tioned here, in a somewhat different light.

God, no doubt, in general, acts, both in the natural and moral world, through the instrumenta-
lity of means. But is it inconsistent with this acknowledgment to believe, that He disposes natural
means in such a manner as to accomplish moral
purposes? Is it unreasonable to suppose that He
who created the universe; who continually pre-
serves it; and who guides all its complicated
movements, foresaw every occurrence, adjusted
every instrument, and interwove with his plan,
from the beginning, every event in the natural
world, which He designed to use, either to re-
ward the righteous, or to punish the wicked?
Consult the scriptures. When war, pestilence,
and famine visited the guilty nations of old, were
they not brought about by natural means, as well
as at the present day? Are we not, at the same
time, assured, that they were instruments of
God's wrath, which He used or withheld according to the character of those with whom He was
dealing? And is He not the same yesterday, to-
day, and forever? If, then, my brethren, you
would altogether escape, or would be visited with
lighter strokes of the rod of affliction, let penitence and reformation go hand in hand with all
our exertions to apply natural preventives, and natural remedies. Without the one, the other can
be of little avail. Nay, I will go farther, without
the one, we have no right to ask for the success

of the other. For it is the solemn declaration of heaven—*The Lord will be with you, while ye be with him ; but if ye forsake him, He will forsake you. Except ye repent, ye shall all likewise perish !*

3. Again, we are called upon this day to mingle trembling with our joy, from a view of the general situation and prospects of the world. It seems to have been with particular reference to this point that the words of our text were originally delivered. It is at the period when God will *dash the nations in pieces, like a potter's vessel,* that we are especially exhorted to *rejoice with trembling.*

If I am not deceived, the Spirit of prophecy informs us, that the days in which we live are the *last days ;* the days in which *perilous times are to come,* the days in which convulsions, disorders, and wickedness are to prevail and triumph more than ever ; the days in which infidelity, moral corruption, national troubles, and various temporal judgments, are to waste the inhabitants of the world, and prepare the way for another generation better fitted to answer the divine purposes. If, with these intimations of prophecy in our hands, we look on the present aspect of human affairs, I apprehend we shall need little argumentation to convince us, that the scriptures are at this moment, most awfully fulfilling. Such a general derangement in the political and moral world, has not, probably, existed since the antediluvian scenes of depravity. And, if we believe the predictions throughout, the corruption and the calamities which we now deplore are but *the beginning of sorrows.* Wars, it is probable, before the Millennium commence, will be more general and sanguinary ; atheism and irreligion more bold in their professions, and more unhinging in their influence ; the whole aspect of human society more deranged and turbid ; and earthquakes, famine, and pestilence more frequent and destructive, than the world has hitherto seen.

I am well aware, that the friends of a certain vain philosophy, falsely so called, will tell me, that these gloomy forebodings are superstitious and visionary. They will tell me that an age of great moral improvement is commenced, and rapidly progressing toward a glorious consummation ; an age in which reason without God, and philosophy without the Gospel, shall purify, tranquilize, and perfect human society. But alas ! where is the proof of this boasted theory ? I ask them whence these happy effects are to originate, and what powerful agency is to produce them ? but I listen in vain for a satisfactory answer. I look abroad, to find the precious fruits of which they speak ; but I see only an ocean every where perturbed, and covered with mist and gloom. I enquire for the harmonizing influence, and the transforming benevolence which they promise to exhibit ; but the passing gale wafts to my ear little else than the noise of war, the collision of vindictive passions, and the groans of misery and death. I listen again, with redoubled attention, for the voice of blessedness, and the sounds of paradise, which they assure me are approaching ; but I hear only the wind and the storm fulfilling the pleasure of the Almighty.

In contemplating this portentous state of things, there would be ground for terror and despair only, were we not assured that Jehovah *rides in the whirlwind, and directs the storm*—that He will bring good out of evil, order out of confusion, light out of darkness, and a kingdom of the greatest glory and blessedness out of materials which are totally depraved. It is only a confidence in the divine government which will warrant us to rejoice in the anticipation of such scenes. But, even with this confidence, who can realize the approach of such *terrible things in righteousness,* without trembling before the God of all the earth ? In this mighty conflict, who that loves his fellow-men, and is concerned for human happiness, can avoid mingling with his ascriptions of praise, the tears of compassion for infatuated mortals, and the humble awe with which these dispensations of heaven are calculated to fill the mind ? *Who shall*

*not fear thee, O Lord, and glorify thy name, when
thy judgments are made manifest?*

Having introduced so many practical remarks,
in stating and illustrating what appeared to be the
doctrine deducible from the text, on the present
occasion, I shall add but little by way of improvement.

I cannot, however, dismiss the subject, without
seriously asking, each individual in this audience,
how they have profited by the solemn dispensation of Providence which they have lately passed
through? Brethren, have you been led by this affliction to consider your ways ; or has it left you
more hardened? Have you been brought by it to
repentance, love, and new obedience ; or has it
made you more secure, careless, and deaf to the
voice of heaven? Have you come out of the furnace purified and refined ; or more full of dross
and corruption than before? Did none of you
make vows and resolutions in the day of adversity?
And are these vows remembered and fulfilled, or
disregarded and forgotten? Have you turned from
your evil way, and put away the accursed thing
from the midst of you ; or is all that guilt which
drew down the judgments of God, still resting in
its dreadful weight upon you? My hearers, these
are not vain questions, they are even your life.
Let me entreat you to answer them without par-

tiality and without evasion ;. for they will be speedily asked before a tribunal where all things will be *naked and open before the eyes of Him with whom we have to do.*

When I look round this populous city, which was, a few weeks since, clothed in mourning, and contemplate the criminal dissipation, and the various forms of wickedness, which have so soon taken the place of those gloomy scenes, I am constrained, with anxious dread, to ask—*Shall not God be avenged on such a people as this ?* Shall he not send greater judgments, and yet greater, in an awful succession, until we either be made to hear his voice, or be utterly consumed before him ? Do not hastily imagine, from this strain of address, that because we have been lately afflicted, it would be my wish to see every innocent amusement discarded, and the gloom and sadness of the pestilential season, still remaining upon every face. By no means. To lighten the cares, and to dispel the sorrows of life, indulging in occasional and innocent amusements is at once our privilege and our duty. But do we see no other than innocent amusements prevailing around us ? Are the lewdness, the blasphemy, the gaming, the unprincipled speculation, the contempt of christian duties, and the violation of the christian sabbath, so mournfully prevalent in our city and land—are these innocent ? Then were the cities of Sodom and Gomorrah innocent. Then are the impious orgies of infernal spirits harmless in the sight of God.

Upon each of us, then, as individuals, there is a task incumbent—the task of *personal reforma- tion and personal holiness*. If it be true that *one sinner destroyeth much good*; it is equally true, that the fervent prayer, and the exemplary virtue of a righteous man avail much. Remember that if there had been ten righteous persons in Sodom, God would have spared the city for their sake. On the same-principle, be assured, that every righteous person in a community adds to its secu- rity, and renders it less probable that Jehovah will visit it with consuming judgments. Let those who are strangers to religion, therefore, be entreated, if they regard their own welfare or that of their country, to return to God with penitence and love through Jesus Christ, and to *walk before him in newness of life*. Sinners! every hour that you continue impenitent, you not only endanger your own souls, but you add to the guilt of the community of which you are members. Awake from your fatal dream! *Behold, now is the accept- ed time ; behold now is the day of salvation ! To- day, if ye will hear his voice, harden not your hearts*. And let the people of God be persuaded, in these solemn times, to grow more watchful, diligent and holy. Christians! *You are the salt of the earth*. The importance of your example, and of your prayers is beyond calculation. If there be any who have an interest at the throne of grace, and who are encouraged to repair to it with an humble boldness, it is YOU. If there be any who are under special obligations to rouse from their lethargy, and to profit by the late awful dispensation, it is YOU. Let the present season, then, form a new æra in your spiritual life. *Be sober and watch unto prayer. Sigh and mourn for all the abominations that are done in the land. For Zion's sake do not hold your peace, and for Jerusalem's sake do not be quiet, until the righteousness thereof go forth as brightness, and the salvation thereof as a lamp that burneth.*

Finally, my brethren, we are exhorted by all that we hear and see—by the word, and by the providence of God, to raise our views above the grovelling pursuits of time and sense ; to live as candidates for immortality ; and to seek an interest in Him who is *the Way, and the Truth, and the Life. What is human life but a vapour, which continueth for a little time, and then vanisheth away ?* Its labours are unsatisfying toils ; its contentions are the jarrings of children ; its hopes are the visions of delirium ; its enjoyments are vanity and vexation of spirit. We are sojourners in a strange land, who tarry but for a night. We wander up and down in a place of graves ; we read the epitaphs on the tombs of the deceased ; we drop a few tears over their precious remains ; and in a little while our friends will be invited to perform the same kind office to us, and to deposit us in the house appointed for all living.—*Lord ! teach us so to number our days, as to apply our hearts unto wisdom.* Help us to grow wiser and better by all thy dealings. And prepare us for that happy world, where there shall be *no more sickness, neither sorrow, nor crying ;* where we shall love and serve thee without the imperfections which cleave to our depraved natures here ; and where we shall *rejoice with joy unspeakable and full of glory !* through riches of free grace in Christ Jesus, to whom with the Father, and the Holy Spirit be glory forever.

AMEN!

NOTES.

P AGE 12.—*Some He saved by providing a place of refuge, &c.*
It is supposed that, at least half the inhabitants of the City
left it. The generous hospitality of our country neighbours,
in receiving many of the fugitives ; and their signal libera-
lity, in contributing to the support of the poor who remained, have already met with many acknowledgments. Too
many they can hardly receive.

It is pleasing to find, that the scruples which were former-
ly prevalent and strong, against flying from pestilence, are
now entertained by few. There seems to be no good reason why those who consider it sinful to retire from a place
under this calamity, should not have the same objection to
flying from famine, from the ravages of fire, or from war,
which are equally judgments of God. And yet those who
reprobate the former, never think of condemning the latter.
In fact, if it be criminal to retire from a city in which the
plague rages, it must be equally criminal to send for a Physician, or to take medicines in any sickness ; for they are
both using means to avert danger to which the Providence
of God has exposed us.* It is hoped, therefore, if Providence should call us to sustain a similar stroke of affliction
in future, there will be a more general agreement than
ever, in the propriety of immediate removal; and that all
will escape without delay, who are not bound to the scene
of danger, by special and indispensible ties. Had all the
inhabitants of New-York remained in the city, during the
late epidemic, probably four or five times the present num-

---

* See Jeremiah 21. 6—9.

ber, on the lowest computation, would have been added to the list of its victims. As every diseased individual or family adds force to the malignity of the atmosphere, it appears that the most benevolent principles conspire with the selfish, in prescribing immediate and general flight.

PAGE 12.—*While others were preserved, though walking in the midst of the devouring poison, to discharge the duties of benevolence and humanity, &c.* In mentioning this description of our citizens, it would be an act of injustice to omit the tribute of grateful acknowledgment to the gentlemen composing the CORPORATION OF THE CITY; to the COMMITTEE OF HEALTH; to the COMMISSIONERS OF THE HEALTH-OFFICE; and to a large number of the PHYSICIANS. Their firmness in remaining at their posts, after the most alarming testimony had been received of the danger to which they were exposed; their disinterested zeal, in discharging the arduous duties committed to them; and their distinguished humanity and benevolence in seeking objects of distress, in entering the cells of poverty, and relieving the wants of the most obscure—it is presumed will be long and gratefully remembered by their fellow-citizens. While the christian blesses God that He moved them to this noble display of virtue, and supported them in it; he will also highly honor *them* as the instruments of saving many lives, and of extensive public utility. To such of the Physicians as remained in the city, until compelled to leave it, by a debility and indisposition, incapacitating them for farther exertions, it is scarcely necessary to say, that the whole of the above acknowledgment is also due. To such of them as fell sacrifices to their benevolence——but alas! the praise of man avails them not. May their memories be long embalmed in the hearts of a grateful people!

PAGE 11.—*When few passengers were seen, save the bearers of, &c.* To those who, with the author, witnessed throughout the melancholy scenes which are here described, this part of the description, at least as it respects a large portion of the city, will appear the unexaggerated, literal truth. The more shocking scenes, which the apartments of the sick presented, he cannot attempt to paint. Even to the present hour, he recollects much of what past before his eyes with shuddering horror.

PAGE 11.—*O Death! how large the catalogue of thy trophies!* &c. The deaths from August 1st. to November 10th. 1798, amounted to more than TWO THOUSAND. Among these were some of the most distinguished ornaments of religion, humanity, and science, which our city afforded. The following list of interments, in each of the burying grounds in the city, within the abovementioned period, may, perhaps, not improperly, be here recorded.

Trinity Church	- - -	214
St. Paul's do.	- - -	211
St. Peter's do.	- - -	86
Christ's do.	- - -	23
United Presbyterian Churches	- -	186
Dutch Reformed	do. - -	129
German Lutheran	do. - -	76
Friend's	do. - -	42
Moravian	do. - - -	3
Methodist	do. - -	79
Baptist	do. - - -	28
Scotch Presbyterian	do. - -	34
Associate Presbyterian do.	- -	10
German Calvinists	do. - -	29
French Protestants	do. - - -	10
Jews	- - -	11
Negroes	- - -	43
Potter's Field	- - -	667
Bellevue	- - -	207
	Total	2082

FINIS.

www.ingramcontent.com/pod-product-compliance
Lightning Source LLC
Chambersburg PA
CBHW021452090426
42739CB00009B/1725